Landmark
insights.

Book 4

Being Up to Something

Published by
Landmark Worldwide
353 Sacramento St., Ste. 200
San Francisco, CA 94111

ISBN-13: 978-0692539958
ISBN-10: 0692539956

Printed in the United States of America
First Edition

This book points out what is possible if we step outside of what we know, and recognize and embrace our capacity to bring forth an entirely new possibility for living—not because it is better, but simply because that is what human beings can do.

New Horizons—The Province of Possibility

The maps we start out with are mostly handed down, inherited with all the peculiarities and standards of our cultures. We often end up living within their parameters, filtering what we see through a somewhat distorted lens. When we accept things as "that's just the way things are," we confine ourselves to those realities—often leading us further from ourselves rather than closer. James Joyce saw maps differently—to paraphrase him, *as errors to arrive at truth.* Errors for him were "volitional," and "portals of discovery"—not a drift through particular landscapes, but a drift through the spaces of the imagination in order to arrive at an invention of reality.

What we do and how we act aren't correlated to "the way things are—a fixed world," but to how the world occurs for us. And they occur that way because that's the conversation we have about them. We mostly don't see the way things are as a product of our conversations (and how those conversations set the values, limitations, and direction of our daily lives) until those conversations are revealed to us as "constructions" that we've put there. When our background conversations shift, the foundational maps on which we construct our understanding of the world shift, too. We feel, think, and act in new ways—fluidity of boundaries is everywhere. Unanticipated directions, surprising connections, new horizons emerge and become the province of possibility.

"Nothing in the horizon limits vision, for the horizon opens all that lies beyond itself." –James Carse

nd itse f. Nothing in the

t lies beyond itself. Nothing in th

orizon limits vision, for t

beyond itself. Nothing in the horiz

orizon opens all that lies

he horizon limits vision, for the h

nd itself. hing in the

he horizon o d that lies beyc

f. Nothi e horizon

beyond elf. ing the horiz

on its on, the l

its or limi

ts visi he horizon

zon limits he horizon

on limi for the h

Stepping Outside of Existing Paradigms, Playing a Bigger Game

A paradigm is a two-edged sword. When we swing it one way, it cuts the information that agrees with it into very fine, precise detail. But when we swing it the other way it will cut us away from information that runs counter to it.[1] In other words, the paradigms we operate from block out specific elements of what we're engaging in, and magnify others. That distorted perspective renders some things possible, some impossible, others not seen at all. We can change things within an existing paradigm and be quite effective, but what we get is only incrementally more of what we already have. Issues arise when who we are, and the environment within which we're operating pushes for something else, when our commitments call for a more expansive landscape, a bigger game.

Stepping outside of an existing paradigm requires questioning our old assumptions, conclusions, decisions, etc—not to get new answers, but to reveal what's possible in being human. It takes a high degree of courage to live with the contradictions between our old views and whole new horizons of living (especially when what we're currently doing may need substantial "undoing"). Human beings aren't genetically encoded with just one way of seeing things or one way of doing things—it's not a matter of finding a better paradigm, but a matter of being able to move among them. It's not a matter of getting rid of our knowledge and experience. it's a matter of getting our blind spots out of the way so there is nothing between us and what we're engaging with. The idea that we have a choice, a say, is a central precept of transformation.

Our Story—Ever Malleable and Open to Being Invented

"…From an early age I knew my ambition was to be in a plot, or several plots—but no plots came my way. You have to apply for them, a friend of mine told me. He'd been around, so I took his advice and went down to the plot factory. Like everything else, there was an interview. 'So,' said the youngish man behind the desk, 'You think you have what it takes to be in a plot? What did you have in mind?'" [2]

When we're asked who we are, we pretty much tell our story. Story telling is key—it's how we understand one another, how we preserve the past, how we make meaning, how we bring new realities to life. While our stories are rich, layered, and unique, we are no more our stories than we are our names, all that happens, the meanings we assign, or our mental or emotional states. The content of our stories is not us—yet, often without us even noticing, the content of our stories and "who we consider ourselves to be" (our identity) get collapsed and become one and the same. The collapse is just kind of a built-in, de facto part of human nature. It's where we get stuck and what immunizes us against the vastness of what's possible in being human.

We can describe and refer to ourselves as "in" the story—to forward our views, launch great ideas, further our commitments—but we are "outside" of it, standing ever ready as the author. Our authorship lives in language. It's in language that we articulate, define, and shape reality, giving us hands-on access to a world that's malleable and always open to being invented.

The Artists of Being Alive

Every day we are presented with opportunities to live as if it's business as usual or to create something exceptional, something beyond who we've been, what we've imagined, and what we know. Each day is a new occasion to express ourselves, to challenge existing options, to set aside current standards, to question firmly held assumptions, to break or even reinvent the mold.

It's with that choice that we begin to get at that spirit so unique, so fundamentally *who we are* that when fully expressed it yields a sheer and spontaneous joy in just being alive—a shift that makes available to us the full possibility of *being* human.

"The most visible creators are those artists whose medium is life itself. The ones who express the inexpressible—without brush, hammer, clay, or guitar. They neither paint nor sculpt. Their medium is simply being. Whatever their presence touches has increased life. They see, but don't have to draw… because they are the artists of being alive…"[3]

THE
ARTISTS
OF BEING
ALIVE

Transformation Carries a Kind of Deep Surprise

Deep surprise is a way we signal ourselves that a thing perceived or thought may be consequential, that a discovery or insight may be of genuine use. What most surprises will be most strongly acted on and most strongly learned, reconfiguring the known for the new. Surprise deepens, gathers, and hones attention to allow a more acute taking-in.[4]

We don't spend much time thinking about what's available to us in being human. But when we do, it's usually about our circumstances, characteristics, traits—our identity. "I am" is the language of identity (*who we consider ourselves to be*). That orientation sets our values, bestows meaning, and determines the purpose and limitations of our daily life. We see the world as if it's "fixed"—obscuring access to ourselves. "I occur," on the other hand, jolts that whole construction and transforms what's available to us in being human.

When we recognize there is no "fixed" world, that it's all an "occurring" world (arising in language), outcomes differ drastically—we begin to see the capacity we have to reach out beyond ourselves. To know the power of language requires a transformation from knowing ourselves as *who we have considered ourselves to be*, and with that shift, identity stops being something that is fixed—our relationship to the world is transformed.

Transformation carries with it that kind of deep surprise. It doesn't merely change our outlook and actions, it uncovers the structures of being and interpretation on which we are grounded. It removes arbitrary views that limit and shape what's possible, and gives us hands-on access to who we are.

Taking the Past Out of the "Future Drawer"

The present is given by the future, but we unwittingly file the past (our many experiences good and bad, how we interpreted them, what we decided about them, the conclusions we made, etc.) into a "future drawer." In doing so, we act, think, and believe as if the present is given by the past.

While it "appears" as if it's the past that's shaping our present-day choices and actions, it really isn't. What actually has the influence is the future we're living into. If we think about it, what inspires us, what moves us, or what stops and defeats us, is directly a function of how we see the future in front of us.

When we recognize that our interpretations of past experiences (and the weight we give them) as well as the futures we're creating are a series of conversations, it becomes clear that we have a choice. We have dominion in the world of saying, giving us hands-on access to a world that's malleable and open to being created.

Communication—Where Life Happens

Communication.

It makes your palms sweat. It makes your stomach tight.

It makes you sigh with relief.

It can alter that way you feel and the way you act.

It's what creates relationships and what can destroy them.

It can make you do things you never thought you'd do

It's something we succeed at one minute and fail at the next.

It sorts out confusion clarifies the mysterious, and has the power
to resolve any breakdown.

It can build bridges and tear down walls.

It's what gives life to our deepest aspirations and our wildest dreams.

It has the power to create and alter the very nature of what is possible.

Mistakes as an Invention Afford Us a Larger Opening

Make mistakes. If you are making mistakes, then you are making new things, trying new things, learning, living… Make glorious, amazing mistakes—mistakes nobody's ever made before. Whatever it is: art, or love, or work or family or life… Make your mistakes.[5]

When we set out to do or be something and we're thwarted or something "goes wrong," there's a disparity between what happened and what the possibility was. But instead of sorting out whatever happened, we often relate to it as some shortcoming, some deficiency about ourselves. Our identity, (who we consider ourselves to be), jumps to front and center. Refrains like "What's wrong with me?" "What's wrong with it?" "What's wrong with 'them'?" are the litanies we hear in our heads. When we operate on top of disempowering assessments, our ability to be gets diminished—it's the "failing to be" that takes us off course, not that "it failed."

If we can consider that what we see as failures (given they live in language) are a making up, an invention, a declaration of something missing, (not necessarily followed by a "therefore" or a "because," but just existing as themselves) instead of a "failure of being," what's there is the possibility of "inventing being." Breakdowns, mistakes, failures as an invention, a saying, a making up, afford us a larger opening—power and freedom have room to emerge.

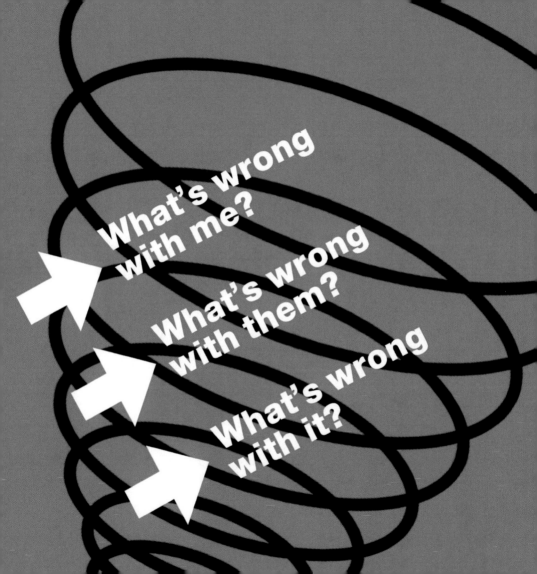

An Excursion into Possibility

Our preferences sometimes tend toward familiarity, safety—but in opting for those we often miss out, even to the point of giving up advancement, intimacy, adventure. We tell ourselves it's easier to avoid something than it is to deal with what can be imagined, created, or committed to. While those decisions might have the "appearance" of freedom, they limit what's possible. When we get wrapped up in our concerns, we can lose sight of what's possible, and essentially adapt to things as they are. Among the major themes to which literature repeatedly turns—love, loss, ambition—none may be richer and more consuming than regret.

When the possibility of power, effectiveness, and freedom arises, there's a concern we might not be able to live up to the possibility. Creating a breakthrough, stepping out, taking new ground requires disrupting our old conversations. There is no right place to begin, but the pull is there to move what we see or imagine as possible into action. Real power occurs when we know we have something to say about the way things are—that we have a voice—that we have access to the state of affairs beyond just reporting on them.

When we invent ourselves by our saying—we begin an excursion into possibility. In Helen Keller's words, "Security is mostly a superstition. Avoiding danger is no safer in the long run than outright exposure. Life is either a daring adventure or nothing."

AN EXCURSION INTO POSSIBILITY.

Create a Future You Really Want and Will Dare to Make Happen

If you hear the word *impossible* or any of its offspring—
unfeasible, impractical, incompatible, unsolvable, insurmountable—
stop everything. And do whatever it takes to eradicate their prefixes.[6]

Create a future that's mapped by the Possible,
A future you really want, and will dare to make happen
…where you ignite your special commitments and passions
…where you're making a difference you're out to make
…where you greet change with a sense of adventure
…where you're a match for the mountain
…where the notion of possibility
moves from an abstract ideal to a day-to-day living reality.

CREATING
THE FUTURE YOU
REALLY WANT

Risking Being Changed by What We Hear

Our inner voice is reassuringly or irritatingly always there on tap, offering us the unfailing, if ambiguous, company of a guest who does not plan to leave.[7] We essentially enter into conversations with some favorable or unfavorable judgment, evaluation, opinions, questions that are already and always at play: "I know" or "I know better," "is it true" or "is it false," "am I going to like/dislike or agree/disagree with what's being said," "is it right or wrong," "is it going to make me look good or bad," etc, etc. There are both *constraining* and *shaping* consequences to coming into conversations with that kind of listening at play. From the *constraining* side, when what's being said by someone is inconsistent with our opinions, we essentially dismiss it in some way and miss out on other views as real possibilities—it constrains our perception. From the *shaping* side, what we walk in with determines the way people and things show up for us. If we think, for example, someone doesn't understand us, like us, respect us, then we become "they don't understand/like/respect me" waiting to happen.

When there is nothing between ourselves and what comes from another person, things don't go through any labyrinth of our evaluations or judgments. In listening without those overlays, in hearing where another person is pointing, we choose to risk being changed by what we hear. A more malleable, fluid world becomes available. The province of possibility emerges, and what it attracts, what we can make happen, has the power to reshape the course of events.

Nothing: an Essential Element
of Transformation

As anyone can tell you, it's a short step from asking, "What does it all mean?" to the inevitable answer, "Nothing." Meaning is constructed by each of us after our own fashion, our own nature; there is no universal formula. True, there is a world out there that would compel us to conform, to consume, to render unto Caesar. But we are, nevertheless, free to furnish our lives with meanings we invent. Henry Miller remarked that "life has to be given meaning because of the obvious fact that is has none" and that "the aim of life is to live, and to live means to be aware, joyously, drunkenly, serenely, divinely aware" leaving us with the capacity to invest life with all the intangible wealth that we can scarcely begin to imagine.[8]

Because we're wired to perceive everything as meaningful, the encounter with *nothing* can be difficult. "Nothing" puts us face-to-face with the malleability of meanings we've held as fundamental to living. To encounter *nothing* as a freedom, we have to pass through and beyond our natural resistance to the very idea. *Nothing*, or *non-being*, is the other side of being; and just as we cannot fully understand light until we have experienced dark, a full openness to what's available in being human calls for an equivalent openness to nothing— an essential element of transformation. Nothing is the foundation for possibility, and in creating possibility, we get to know what's possible in being human.

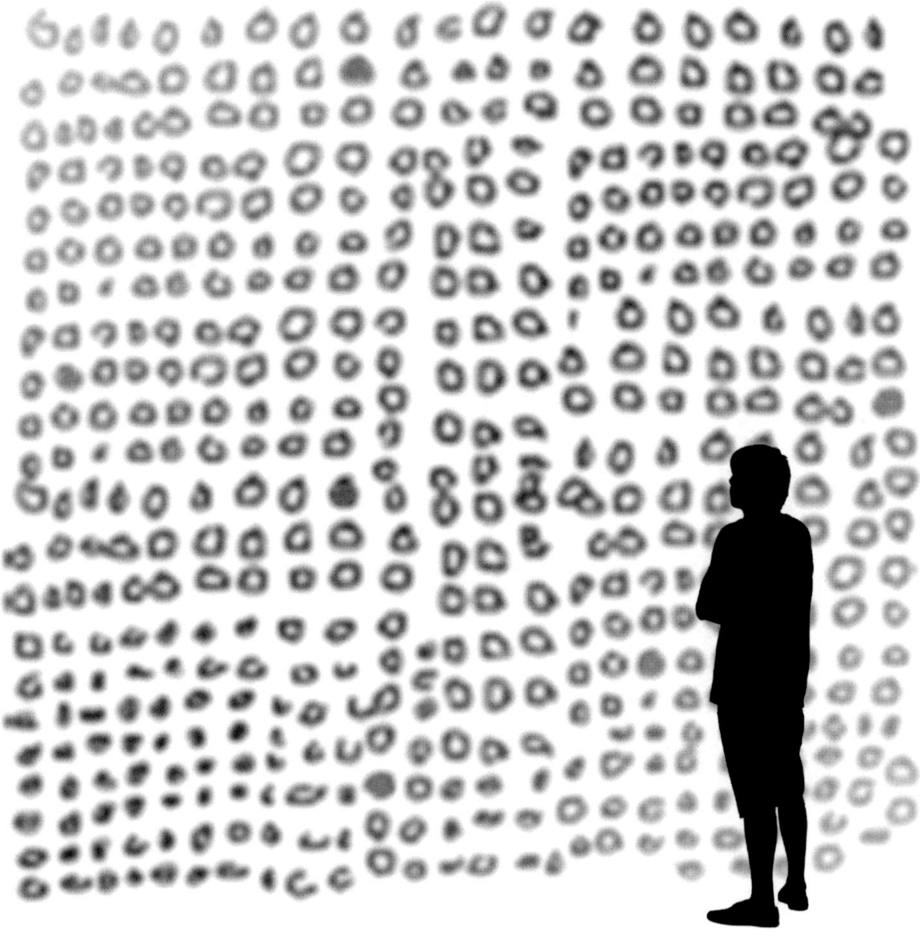

Being Up to Something

What marks a visionary is dedication to a possibility, a dedication that rejects outright the complacency of those who prefer the status quo and insists that there has to be another way. Instead of reaching for the nearest, most convenient conclusions, their commitment causes them to push hard against the limits of what others might see as possible.[9]

When we are up to something, we are called to step forward, to be and act in wholly new ways, to risk what we already know for something beyond the predictable. To be up to something calls forth strength and creativity—it generates energy and excitement that attracts and invites the participation of others. When we are up to something, we step outside the constraints of our circumstances, and stand for a possibility. We don't reference what's possible against who we've been or what's been done in the past, what's predictable or expected, but rather against what we stand for and see as possible. Conditions and circumstances begin to reorder and realign themselves inside of what we stand for. Our relationship to possibility moves from an abstract ideal or remote objective to a viable, living reality.

BEING UP TO SOMETHING

Endnotes

1. Joel Barker

2. Adapted from Margaret Atwood, *The Tent* (Anchor Books, 2007).

3. Donna J. Stone

4. Adapted from Jane Hirshfield, *Ten Windows: How Great Poems Transform the World* (Knopf, 2015).

5. Adapted from Neil Gaiman, *My New Year Wish* (neilgaiman.com, 2011).

6. Adapted from Bull HN Information Systems, Inc

7. Adapted from Denise Riley, *The Inner Voice* (Harper's Magazine, 2005).

8. Adapted from John Burnside, *The Big Question: What's the Point?* (Intelligent Life magazine, 2014).

9. Adapted from Denise Shekerjian, *Uncommon Genius* (Viking Penguin, 1990).

Made in the USA
Middletown, DE
28 June 2023

34109320R00020